DON'T MENTION MY NAME

A New Comedy in Two Acts

by Fred Carmichael

SAMUEL FRENCH, INC.
45 WEST 25TH STREET   NEW YORK 10010
7623 SUNSET BOULEVARD HOLLYWOOD 90046
LONDON   TORONTO

ii

IMPORTANT BILLING AND CREDIT REQUIREMENTS

All producers of DON'T MENTION MY NAME *must* give credit to the Author of the Play in all programs distributed in connection with performances of the Play and in all instances in which the title of the Play appears for purposes of advertising, publicizing or otherwise exploiting the Play and/or a production. The name of the Author *must* also appear on a separate line, on which no other name appears, immediately following the title, and *must* appear in size of type not less than fifty percent the size of the title type.

CHARACTERS

SYLVIA DUTTON

DEXTER CHANDLER

VERLA PERKINS

MAN

JANE RIDGELY

KITTY CARSON

PAUL MILES

WILMA CHANDLER

TIME & PLACE

The action of the play takes place in the living room of a Bed and Breakfast Inn in Vermont.

ACT I
Early evening of the present.

ACT II

Scene 1
Immediately following.
Scene 2
Later the same evening.

DON'T MENTION MY NAME

ACT I

SCENE: The action of the play takes place in the living room of a large country Bed and Breakfast Inn. The room is modern and very comfortable. D.R. is a door to the outside and directly above it is a window. On the U.R. wall there is a shallow coat closet and C. of that is a wide opening through which stairs can be seen leading off U.R. to the upstairs, U.L. leads to the kitchen. There is a bathroom door on the U.L. wall and to the L. of that are corner bookshelves filled with books and TV video tapes. D.L. is a door which leads to a bar and game room and through that also to the kitchen. Below the shelves there is a desk with a desk chair above it, a straight chair to its R. and a backless bench below it. A sofa is stage R. with a small table to its R. The general appearance of the room is one of comfort and expense in decor. It is a New England October evening but still warm out. MOONLIGHT comes through the window which floods the stage with a blue wash.

AT RISE: A FLASHLIGHT appears at the window and then the faces of SYLVIA DUTTON and DEXTER CHANDLER. SHE is a professional

office woman and is dressed accordingly.
THEY are both in their thirties or forties and
HE is definitely an executive and wears
comfortable sport coat and slacks.

SYLVIA. I tell you it is closed.

DEXTER. It can't be.

SYLVIA. It is dark. It is deserted. It is closed.

DEXTER. Maybe he's out. Maybe the door's open.

SYLVIA. And maybe there's a Santa Claus.

DEXTER. (*Rattles door handle.*) It's locked.

SYLVIA. Look what you're standing on.

DEXTER. What?

SYLVIA. The mat.

DEXTER. It says welcome.

SYLVIA. So? The key is always under the mat.

DEXTER. Don't be silly. No one leaves the key under the—oh!

SYLVIA. Now put the key in the lock and then we will be entering but not breaking in.

DEXTER. (*Sound of KEY in lock and door opens.*) No hotel should be closed.

SYLVIA. (*Comes in carrying flashlight and purse.*) This is not a hotel. It is a Bed and Board.

DEXTER. (*Enters with key and pencil flashlight in hand.*) Bed and Breakfast.

SYLVIA. (*Laughs.*) You look like the hall porter. Put the key down.

DEXTER. Where?

SYLVIA. Where it belongs, under the mat.

DEXTER. (*HE does so, comes in and closes door.*) This is all very odd.

SYLVIA. And nerve-wracking. The dark is no help. There must be a light switch somewhere. (*Shines light D.R.*) Aha, here.

DEXTER. No, the flashlight's enough.

SYLVIA. Are you saying Thomas Edison wasted his time? I want electric light. (*Starts for light switch D.R.*)

DEXTER. (*Blocks her way.*) He'll know we're here.

SYLVIA. You did make a reservation? (*Pause.*) Dexter Chandler, you did make a reservation? (*Pause.*) You didn't.

DEXTER. I forgot.

SYLVIA. (*Crosses C.*) Now what?

DEXTER. (*Moves to her.*) He must be out getting supplies, you know things like Aunt Jemima's Waffle Mix and syrup, good old Vermont maple syrup maybe tapped from the very tree we parked under.

SYLVIA. That tree around the corner happens to be an elm. Why don't you get the car and bring in the bags? (*Starts to sit on sofa and stops.*) I'll wait here. No, I won't, not in the dark.

DEXTER. If anyone sees a light they might come and investigate and they might not be Roger Lenox.

SYLVIA. (*Goes to him.*) It could be the police.

DEXTER. Or a private detective.

SYLVIA. Or your wife.

DEXTER. Shh!

SYLVIA. (*Crosses up and looks through hallway and then moves D.L.*) You're sure this Lenox doesn't know Wilma?

DEXTER. (*Meets her below bench.*) You don't know her. No one in the office does, not even Jason Meadows and he guaranteed this place.

SYLVIA. Where is this Lenox? I'm getting nervous.

DEXTER. (*Goes to front door.*) We'd better wait for him in the car. We can have a cigarette.

SYLVIA. I gave up smoking and so did you.

DEXTER. Then we can chew a fat-free Granola bar.

SYLVIA. (*Peeks through door D.L.*) Look at this. It's a sort of game room with card tables and a small bar. Let's have a drink.

DEXTER. We'd better go before—

SYLVIA. (*Points to door U.R.*) What's in there, a john?

DEXTER. (*Opens door.*) Probably or a downstairs guest room. No, it's just a coat closet.

(*From offstage outside we hear VERLA PERKINS singing a few bars of SHINE ON HARVEST MOON.*)

VERLA. "Shine on, shine on Harvest Moon for me and my gal" ... here we are.

DEXTER. Good. Roger is here.

SYLVIA. That is a woman's voice.

DEXTER. Oh, God. Hide. Quick.

SYLVIA. Where?

DEXTER. There. (*Points to bar as HE goes into closet.*)

SYLVIA. Good. I get the bar.

(*THEY both close doors as VERLA PERKINS enters after we hear the KEY in the lock. VERLA is a very large and strong country woman who tends to the place. SHE is blunt but not stupid even though a bit slow at times.*)

VERLA Under the mat. How original. (*Puts the key back under the mat and reaches down to pick up a pile of towels and washcloths all washed and folded. Some are flowered and some are striped and some are solid colors. SHE puts on the LIGHTS and closes the door. SHE goes to the bathroom and opens the door, stops and leaves one set of towels on the desk and starts again for bathroom.*) Oh, no way. Wrong color. (*Starts to match colors and stops.*) Oh, the hell with it. Them city folks don't have to have them match. Let them rough it. (*Goes into bathroom singing again as DEXTER sticks his head out of closet, crosses D.L. and SYLVIA opens barroom door.*)

SYLVIA. (*Whispers.*) Oh, it's you.

DEXTER. Someone's in there.

SYLVIA. I can hear.

DEXTER. It is not Roger Lenox.

SYLVIA. What'll we do?

DEXTER. Leave and come back later.

SYLVIA. Hurry.

(VERLA's offstage singing gets louder.)

DEXTER. Too late. *(Pushes her through D.L. door with him as VERLA enters.)*

VERLA. *(Gets rest of towels from desk.)* Towels is towels, ain't they? *(As SHE goes upstairs.)* Color don't make no difference. All get dirty anyways. This ain't no Quality Inn.

DEXTER. *(Pulls SYLVIA out as VERLA exits.)* Come on, out the back way.

SYLVIA. *(Stops and looks at the room.)* This place is much nicer in the light. I'm going to enjoy this weekend.

DEXTER. If we ever get to it.

SYLVIA. *(Heads for bathroom.)* I want to look at the towels.

DEXTER. *(Grabs her again.)* Later.

SYLVIA. I'm hungry.

DEXTER. Candy bar is in the car.

SYLVIA. *(As THEY leave through hallway and U.L.)* You have a cellular phone. Can't we send out for Chinese?

VERLA. *(Comes in as THEY exit.)* Hello. Someone here? *(Goes to window.)* Thought I heard voices. *(Looks out.)* No one. That car around the corner. *(Puts LIGHTS off.)* That bears investigation. Out the back way and skirt around. *(Goes U.C.)* What do they say? The game's afoot. *(Exits out hallway.)*

(At the window we see a MAN'S face, HE looks in and then KNOCKS on door.)

MAN. Someone? Anyone there? Someone, please help. (*NOISE of a flower pot breaking.*) Damn! I broke your—oh, a key. (*KEY is heard in lock and the door opens and MAN enters. HE is a man in his thirties, nice looking but not distinguished in any way. HE wears a sports coat and slacks and open-necked shirt. HE is rather messed and carries the flower pot in one hand and the geranium and roots in another along with the key.*) Hello ... I broke your geranium. It fell on the mat and I found the key and—(*Looks around.*) Who the hell am I talking to anyway? Lights? Where are the lights? (*Sees switch and flicks it and the LIGHTS go on.*) There. (*Calls.*) Hello, I just want to use your phone. (*Listens a moment.*) Sorry about the geranium. (*Puts it back in pot.*) Maybe it'll rain and it will be all right. (*Puts it outside again and the key under the mat.*) The key under the mat. How original. (*Comes back in and closes door. HE is exhausted and leans against door.*) Oh, boy! (*His hand to his head and then feels in his pockets.*) No handkerchief. No license. No wallet. I got plenty of nothing. That's from *Porgy and Bess*. If I can remember that why can't I remember who I am? Ohhh, my head! A cloth, a cold cloth, that's what I need. (*Opens closet door.*) A closet! (*Goes U.C.*) There must be water somewhere. Oh, the country. They must have an indoor outhouse. (*Goes into bathroom U.L.*) Ah, I'm not in Death Valley after all. My head! Something cool for my head. Oh, that feels better.

(*Comes out with cloth to forehead and collapses on bench below desk.*) Test the patient for brain damage, that's what they always do. (*Holds one finger in front of his face.*) One finger. (*Holds up two fingers.*) Two fingers. (*Holds up three.*) Wait, I know the answers. I'm holding up the fingers. What day is it? Friday. What month is it? October. When was the Magna Carta signed? 1215. I know that so why don't I know who I am? (*Crosses U.C.*) There are mountains outside and I am in the U.S. unless they have taken my passport and I am in Tibet. Then I'd be a man without a country. Am I Nathan Hale? No, my jacket is Brooks Brothers. (*Sees phone on desk.*) The phone. In an emergency dial 911. (*HE does.*) Thank you, Ma Bell or whichever subsidiary you are. Hello ... yes an emergency, a missing person.... The local police? Right. (*Hangs up and dials "O" and sits at desk.*) Operator, give me the police ... what town? The one I am in. Wait a minute, there's a phone book here. (*Looks in it.*) Twin Rivers, is that possible?... You do? A cousin?... I doubt if I know him. Can you connect me with the local police, the sheriff, the posse, anyone?.. What?... Oh, thank you, the odds are against it but I'll certainly try to have a nice day. (*Looks at size of phone book which is very thin.*) Population of Twin Rivers must be 125 if they're all at home ... Hello, police? Please connect me with the Missing Persons Bureau ... You don't? What do you do when someone's missing?... Oh, you do the best you can. I see. Do you have a report of a missing person?... Description? (*Rises and looks from floor up trying to measure himself.*) About six feet. Rather handsome, I hope. Hang on a minute. (*Rushes into bathroom and returns with small hand mirror.*) Scratch that. Medium handsome and that may be a bit on the optimistic side. (*ACTOR then describes himself basically and what he is wearing.*) No identifiable scars. Got that? Please call if there is any news. I'll stay right here. (*Looks at number on phone.*) 866-4225.... My name? Oh, it's—it's (*Grabs book from shelves and reads author's name.*) ... Emerson, Ralph Waldo ... No, just a distant relative ... Thank you. (*Hangs up and puts book back.*) Why did I pick that book? Why not Harold Robbins or Stephen King or even Danielle Steel? (*Picks up cloth.*) Now, wash my face and wait. My memory will come back like my VCR on rerun. (*H E exits.*)

(*JANE's face appears at the window, SHE KNOCKS on the door. Pause and KEY is heard in lock and SHE opens door and pokes her head in. SHE is in her late twenties, attractive and dressed casually.*)

JANE. Hello. (*Pause.*) Water's running. (*Runs toward bathroom just as MAN comes out and THEY almost collide.*) Oh.
MAN. Yes, oh.
JANE. You're early.
MAN. I am?

JANE. You said tomorrow.

MAN. And here it is today.

JANE. Yes. (*After an awkward pause.*) I am Jane Ridgely.

MAN. Oh?

JANE. From the real estate office.

MAN. Oh, yes.

JANE. I'd better put the key back. (*SHE does and comes back in closing the door.*) It was under the mat for you but I guess you found it.

MAN. Yes, I did.

JANE. Keys are always under mats, aren't they?

MAN. Yes. Always.

JANE. (*Talking fast and nervously, SHE efficiently shows him the room.*) That's a closet up there and (*Goes to bathroom.*) you found this bathroom (*Goes U.L. and then down to barroom door.*) and down here is a game room and bar for your guests.

MAN. (*Crosses down.*) My guests?

JANE. You rent a place this big for a week and of course you're going to have guests.

MAN. Of course.

JANE. Since it's a Bed and Breakfast in season it is well equipped.

MAN. Great.

JANE. (*Goes U.C.*) There are eating supplies in the kitchen. That's through there or (*Goes D.L.*) down here, either way. Any questions?

MAN. Just one. I don't know who—

JANE. (*Goes to him.*) Of course. You don't know where the lease is. It was so late when you called we couldn't mail it.

MAN. Yes, but—

JANE. I was planning on bringing it as soon as you got here tomorrow but then I saw the lights on and, well, I thought I was wrong on the date but I'm not, am I?

MAN. Probably not.

JANE. I'm new at this. I just started. I'll run down to the office and bring the lease back right away. (*Runs to door and opens it.*) Oh, I forgot. I'm Jane Ridgely, but then I said that, didn't I?

MAN. Yes.

JANE. Do you want the lease made out to John or Jack?

MAN. John or Jack?

JANE. Yes. Is Jack a nickname or official?

MAN. Oh, Jack is fine.

JANE. Great. Then it's Jack Lister. (*Closes door leaving him in a state of confusion.*)

MAN. Is it Jack Lister? John Lister? Jack Lister? So he has this place for a week. Or I have it. Me? No, he. I don't feel very Jack Lister. The phone book. (*Goes to desk.*) No, I'm obviously from out of town. (*Sees answering machine on desk.*) Aha! An answering machine. A clue. (*Presses button on it.*)

VOICE OVER MICROPHONE. (*The Voice is a gruff, uncultured one, very low and ominous.*) You know who this is ... tonight's the pick-up. The package is ready so you better be ready or don't plan on reading Sunday's papers. You'll be in the obituary.

MAN. Me?

VOICE. (*Continues without interruption.*) And I do mean you. (*Clicks off.*)

MAN. I thought so. (*Winds machine back.*) If he means me I am in big trouble. If he doesn't mean me and I don't have the package I am still in big trouble. It is time for a hasty exit. (*Heads for front door.*) Obituary? Package? I don't have any package. I don't have (*Opens door and VERLA stands there holding pile of sheets and pillowcases freshly ironed. MAN'S voice goes soft.*) anything.

VERLA. No problem. I have everything. (*Comes into room past him.*) I have everything. Washed and ironed them myself. Hung them outdoors, too. Makes them sunshine fresh like the ads say. Here, smell. (*Holds them up to him while HE sniffs.*)

MAN. Hmm, nice.

VERLA. Better than them smelly paper sheets you put in the dryer, ain't they? (*SHE looks at him.*) Well, ain't they?

MAN. Definitely. (*Closes the front door.*)

VERLA. I wasn't expectin' you tonight or I'd have done these afore now. I seen your lights on so I got them out of my truck. I thought that was your car around the corner but it's gone now. How'd you get here?

MAN. Well, I—how do you think one would get here?

VERLA. Joe's taxi?

MAN. Right you are. He's a good driver.

VERLA. She. Jo is short for Josephine.

MAN. She sure has a low voice.

VERLA. In the church choir she's the bass. (*Goes U.C.*) I better get to the beds. Anything you want, just let me know, Mr. Roderman.

MAN. Roderman?

VERLA. That's right, ain't it?

MAN. (*Moves upstage*) How do you know it?

VERLA. The real estate office.

MAN. They didn't tell you I was Jack Lister?

VERLA.They said Milton Roderman.

MAN. Milton Roderman.

VERLA. (*Goes to him.*) If you want to be called Jack Lister, it's OK with me. Lotsa men don't want to use their real names on these short rentals. (*Nudges him.*) I understand.

MAN. Good.

VERLA. How many beds shall I make up?

MAN. (*Giving up, goes R. of sofa.*) Who knows? Make them all.

VERLA. There's a heap of rooms up there, but the more the merrier. By the way, I'm Verla. I guess you figured I do for you.

MAN. Me?

VERLA. Whoever's here. (*SHE turns to go upstairs.*)

MAN. (*Crosses below sofa.*) Verla.

VERLA. Yeah.

MAN. Perhaps you can help. I called the sheriff's office but he was off duty. When is he on duty?

VERLA. I'd say in about an hour.

MAN. How do you know?

VERLA. He'll be back soon as he finishes makin' the beds. I'm the sheriff. (*Goes upstairs.*)

MAN. (*Looking after her.*) The sheriff? I am in big trouble. Lister? Roderman? No, neither fits. The package doesn't fit either. (*Heads for front door.*) I'm outta here. I am history. (*Stops at door.*) No one better be outside that door. One, two—(*Opens door and JANE has her hand up to knock.*)

JANE. Hi.

MAN. (*Weakly.*) Three.

JANE. (*Comes in below him.*) Mr. Lister, I am back and I am stupid.

MAN. (*Closes door.*) Are you?

JANE. I clean forgot the office is closed and I left my key in my desk drawer.

MAN. Yes.

JANE. (*Thinking of a reason to stay.*) So we're both at loose ends. How about my making a cup of coffee?

MAN. Sure, why not?

JANE. (*Goes U.C.*) I'll put the water on. Is instant all right?

MAN. Sure.

JANE. Regular or decaff?

MAN. (*Goes U.C.*) Straight and strong. I have a feeling it's going to be a long night.

JANE. Yes. (*Exits down hallway.*)

MAN. (*Looks at machine.*) Roderman? Lister? (*Turns on machine.*) Let's try again.

VOICE. (*Repeat of same message.*) You know who this is—

MAN. I don't, I tell you.

VOICE. tonight's the pickup—

MAN. Of what?

VOICE. The package is ready—

MAN. What package?

VOICE. ... so you better be ready or don't plan on reading Sunday's paper.

MAN and VOICE TOGETHER. You'll be in the Obituary.

MAN. Not me.

VOICE. And I do mean you. (*Clicks off.*)

MAN. He means Lister or Roderman but not— whoever I am.

JANE. (*Rushes in through bar D.L.*) Water's on. (*Looks about quickly.*) Who was here? I heard voices.

MAN. That was the answering machine. (*Testing her, HE goes to L. of desk.*) They wanted a Milton Roderman.

JANE. I don't know any Milton Roderman.

MAN. Must be a wrong number.

JANE. (*Crosses D.C.*) We get a lot of them out here in the country. (*Pause while HE looks at her.*) A lot.

MAN. So you just started with the real estate company?

JANE. Yes, just. (*Another awkward pause.*) This week in fact.

MAN. (*Moves in below bench.*) And you live around here or you just got here?

JANE. (*Brightly.*) Yes.

MAN. Which?

JANE. Which what?

MAN. Live here or just got here?

JANE. Both.

MAN. How's that?

JANE. (*Moves away R.*) I just got here and I live around here now.

MAN. Oh. (*Goes to her below sofa.*) Is it a hard test?

JANE. What?

MAN. To get a real estate license.

JANE. Yes and no.

MAN. Which?

JANE. No for me and yes for someone with an IQ of 38. (*Laughs as SHE goes below him to C.*) What do you do, Mr. Lister?

MAN. Oh, call me Jack.

JANE. Jack.

MAN. (*Lying.*) I'm in real estate, too, in the city. Biggest firm actually. Boy, the prices on those condos are something, aren't they?

JANE. Yes, really something.

MAN. We must sit down and have a long talk about contracts and the legal end of it.

JANE. Oh, the water must be boiling. (*Rushes out U.C.*) I'll be right back.

MAN. (*With a look after her.*) Real estate, ha! (*Goes below sofa.*) Who the hell is she and why, but then who the hell am I and why?

VERLA. (*Comes downstairs.*) Mr. Roderman. (*MAN looks around to see who she means.*) Mr. Roderman—

MAN. Oh, me, yes.

VERLA. (*Goes to him.*) How fussy are your friends?

MAN. Pardon me.

VERLA. The ones what's visitin'. My colors ain't matchin' in towels and face rags.

MAN. I'm sure they won't mind.

VERLA. I put some plaid towels with some flowered face rags.

MAN. Sounds psychedelic.

VERLA. I'm better at bein' the sheriff than the chambermaid. Give me a drug pusher or a mugger and I know what to do. (*Does a karate stance and a violent kick out.*) Hi-ya!

MAN. Black belt?

VERLA. No belts, just fists and feet.

MAN. I believe it.

VERLA. If you was a crook I could take you and break you in two. (*SHE descends on him.*) You believe that?

MAN. Implicitly.

JANE. (*Comes in with two cups of coffee.*) Sugar? Milk? (*Sees Verla.*) Oh.

MAN. Just black.

VERLA. (*Goes to her.*) How do. You must be Mrs. Roderman.

JANE. No, I'm—

VERLA. Then you two are—what do they call it?—having a serious relativeship— relationship—whatever?

MAN. Why, this is Jane Ridgely. You must know her.

VERLA. Don't.

JANE. I don't think we—

MAN. (*Goes below Verla to Jane, gets cup of coffee and goes to the bench.*) But she works in the real estate office and you do houses for them don't you?

JANE. The phone. (*To Verla.*) We must have spoken on the phone.

VERLA. Nope.

JANE. I'm sure we did.

VERLA. Two things I never forget, a voice and Groundhog's Day.

MAN. Groundhog's Day?

VERLA. It's also my birthday.

(*MAN sits on bench.*)

JANE. I haven't worked at the office for long.

VERLA. I was in there three times last week and no you.

JANE. (*Sits next to Man.*) Of course, it's my hair.

MAN. What is?

JANE. It was very long last week and then, on a whim, I had it cut and the color changed.

VERLA. Looks natural to me.

JANE. Well, it ain't—isn't.

VERLA. If you know me, what's my name?

MAN. (*After JANE pauses.*) I'm terrible at names, too.

VERLA. Would you believe Verla?

JANE. You won't catch me that way. Ten dollars says no one is named Verla.

VERLA. You lose.

MAN. Do you take American Express?

VERLA. Where's the ten?

MAN. You trapped us, Verla. This lady is my wife.

JANE. I am?

VERLA. What?

JANE. (*Definitely.*) I am!

MAN. (*His arm around her.*) We're keeping it a secret—We're on our honeymoon.

VERLA. Then why are you havin' all these people come fill the beds I'm makin'?

JANE. It's my mother.

VERLA. She comin' on your honeymoon?

MAN. I hope not.

JANE. She told all our friends we'd be here so we know they'll surprise us.

VERLA. Some friends. (*Goes to stairs.*) Well, I'll finish up the beds and then towels and then leave you two alone. Honeymoons is nice. Been on three myself. No, four, but then I don't count Calvin. He keeled over dead and we was married less than one night. (*Goes upstairs.*)

MAN. I'm not going to touch that one.

JANE. (*Crosses below sofa.*) You knew I was lying.

MAN. You were getting in deep all right.

JANE. Why did you save me?

MAN. I don't really know. You look so trustworthy, like a Boy Scout.

JANE. Girl Scout. (*Puts cup on table by sofa.*)

MAN. (*Smiles.*) Of course.

JANE. I do work at the office but only part time. I started yesterday and—

(*PHONE rings.*)

MAN. Hold it, the phone. (*HE puts cup on desk and and crosses C.*) We can hear who left the message on the answering machine.

JANE. (*Goes to him.*) No, shut it off. Don't listen.

MAN. (*Goes to machine.*) But it's before we got here so who did it?

JANE. No, please, it's—

MAN. Listen—

(*JANE's voice comes on the machine but she is using a rather tough accent.*)

JANE'S VOICE. Yeah—you got 866-4225. I'm leavin' this message for you-know-who because he don't make recordings.

MAN. (*Looking at her.*) Jane—

JANE'S VOICE. He said to tell you it's here tonight. Don't be late with the package. You got somethin' to say, wait for the damn beep.

MAN. That's you. That voice is yours.

(Sound of BEEP from machine.)

JANE. I can explain.

MAN. Listen—

(MALE voice on machine, same one as before.)

VOICE. My contact should be there by now. Hand the money over or plan on broken arms, broken legs, and a neck that ain't too straight. Get me?

MAN. Is he talking to you?

VOICE. And I am talkin' to you. *(Clicks off.)*

MAN. Well?

JANE. *(Goes below sofa.)* I find myself in a rather awkward position.

MAN. You were auditioning for the community theatre production of *Guys and Dolls*?

JANE. *(Sits on sofa.)* Let's sit down.

MAN. *(Goes to sofa.)* Am I going to believe this?

JANE. It may seem far-fetched.

MAN. *(Sits beside her.)* Whatever it is, I can top it.

JANE. I am not what you think.

MAN. That's obvious.

JANE. What do you think I am?

MAN. I think you are not who you say you are and you are not in the real estate office and you are about to tell me the truth finally and, most of all, I think you are very lovely.

JANE. (*Flustered.*) That is beside the point.

MAN. Not necessarily. We just got married.

JANE. Are you always this flip?

MAN. I don't know about "always," but back to your story.

JANE. Between that answering machine and Verla up there I didn't get away with much. I am a private investigator.

MAN. And I am Jimmy Hoffa.

JANE. (*Rises and crosses to window and looks out.*) I really am a P.I. I've just been hired by the government.

MAN. Ours?

JANE. Of course ours.

MAN. I hope ours is also mine.

JANE. Why shouldn't it be?

MAN. Thereby hangs a tale.

JANE. (*Crosses up and glances up the stairs.*) Tonight an ongoing investigation is going to climax.

MAN. You mean here?

JANE. (*Moves D.C.*) Exactly.

MAN. Right here?

JANE. We have every reason to think so.

MAN. Do I believe you?

JANE. That's what I should be asking. Do you believe me?

MAN. (*Rises and goes to her at C.*) Why should I? What is this investigation?

JANE. (*Goes D.L. and glances into barroom.*) It all started with an informer. He was granted immunity for certain information. He said the government could catch someone they really wanted red-handed here tonight.

MAN. Who?

JANE. That was all the informer would say until he was guaranteed his release.

MAN. So he's out now?

JANE. No.

MAN. Why not?

JANE. (*Goes to him.*) His last night in prison he went to the movies.

MAN. The damn fool. A knife, right? A shiv in the back and when the lights came up he was dead. He should have known.

JANE. (*Goes below him to sofa.*) So all we know is that something is going to go down here tonight.

MAN. And you've come to prevent it?

JANE. Or to see who shows up to do what.

MAN. (*Crosses in below sofa.*) And the phone call?

JANE. (*Sits on sofa.*) That confirms everything, doesn't it?

MAN. (*Sits beside her.*) But why did you make that message?

JANE. For the Big Boy to hear. I broke in here earlier. I failed with my lock pick and then I found the key under the mat. That's how stupid I am.

MAN. So what happens if I believe you?

JANE. Are you a loyal citizen?

MAN. True blue.

JANE. Then tell me about yourself, just the short version.

MAN. It'll be short all right.

JANE. Go on.

VERLA. (*Calls from upstairs.*) Soap!

MAN. It's Verla.

JANE. (*Whispers.*) We can't trust her. We can't trust anyone. Quick. Pretend we're on our honeymoon.

MAN. But I—

JANE. It's for our government. (*Grabs him in a passionate kiss.*)

VERLA. (*Has come downstairs.*) Comin' through. 'Scuse me.

JANE. (*Breaks kiss but THEY stay wrapped in each other's arms.*) Verla!

MAN. We were just—

VERLA. Soap. I need soap for the bathrooms. There's some in the pantry. Don't mind me. You two go on enjoyin' yourselves. (*Exits down hallway.*)

MAN. (*In a daze.*) She is getting soap.

JANE. (*Also in a daze.*) So she said.

MAN. We'd better go on pretending.

JANE. Should we?

MAN. As you said, it's for our government.

(THEY kiss as VERLA walks through with bars of soap.)

VERLA. *(Turns at foot of stairs and watches them with a sigh.)* Be careful you two. That's what killed my Calvin. *(Goes upstairs.)*

MAN. *(As THEY break.)* Say, I like being married to you. Let's not keep it a secret any longer.

JANE. *(Pushes him away slightly.)* Don't get carried away. We hardly know each other. All I know about you is you're not supposed to be here and I made up your name of Jack Lister.

MAN. All I know about me is I am not Jack Lister.

JANE. Then you might be—*(Suddenly it hits her.)* are you here to pick up the package? Oh, my God, my gun is in my purse. I've had it. My first job and I am dead meat.

MAN. Hang on, I'm not the criminal. I'm sure I'm not. Do I look like a felon.

JANE. No.

MAN. Do I kiss like a felon?

JANE. I don't know how a felon kisses but you do it very nicely.

MAN. So do you. *(Starts to kiss her but SHE stops him.)*

JANE. Why didn't you stop me when I called you Jack Lister?

MAN. It's as good a name as any.

JANE. Who are you?

MAN. (*Whispers as HE moves in for a kiss.*) I don't know.

JANE. (*After a small kiss.*) Everyone knows who he is.

MAN. (*After another small kiss.*) I don't.

JANE. (*Breaks mood.*) You are kidding, aren't you?

MAN. Nope.

JANE. You don't want to tell me anything because I'm an investigator, right?

MAN. Wrong. I honestly do not know who I am or rather who I was.

JANE. Was when?

MAN. An hour, two hours ago. I believe you so how about you believing me?

JANE. You've blown my cover and saved me from that cavewoman with the soap so try me. What is your story?

MAN. I know everything except two things.

JANE. Which are?

MAN. Who I am and what I am doing here.

JANE. Those are two biggies.

MAN. I know what day it is. I can recite the alphabet. I can count up to ten and—(*JANE holds up two fingers.*) Skip that. I tried it. I succeeded. (*Rises and moves U.C.*) The first thing I remember is walking down the road outside. I have no I.D. on me, not a wallet, not a license, not even a penny. My head hurt so I must have fallen down.

JANE. Or had an accident.

MAN. Or been mugged. This was the first house I came to after walking for what seemed miles. No one was here but—

JANE. The key was under the mat.

MAN. Yes.

JANE. (*Crosses up top of him.*) Maybe your subconscious led you here and you are the felon.

MAN. I could be from the government like you. In fact, I could be superior to you.

JANE. No, you're too incompetent.

MAN. Verla calls me Milton Roderman, says the real estate office gave her the name but I don't feel like Milton Roderman.

JANE. Whoever you are, we'd better work together until we find out if you're good or bad.

MAN. (*Sits in chair R. of desk.*) If I am the criminal then I apologize.

JANE. Thank you. (*Paces.*) What do you suppose one does for amnesia?

MAN. Hit me on the head again.

JANE. That might kill you.

MAN. Kiss me again. That might cure me.

JANE. We tried that.

MAN. Who am I?

JANE. The World Almanac!

MAN. No. Maybe I'm Webster's Unabridged. but I am not—

JANE. (*Goes to shelves crossing above desk.*) Let's see what the Almanac says about amnesia.

MAN. (*Goes to her via L. of desk.*) You are clever.

JANE. There must be a reference book here somewhere.

MAN. There's a book by Ralph Waldo Emerson.

JANE. (*As SHE looks through books.*) We could call someone.

MAN. I tried that.

JANE. If there's a hot line for overeaters and a hot line for oversmokers, there must be one for amnesiacs.

MAN. But we'd have forgotten who to call.

JANE. Here we are. (*Pulls out large book from bottom shelf.*) A medical encyclopedia. You look it up. It starts with A.

MAN. (*As HE looks it up.*) I told you I remembered the alphabet.

JANE. What a library; romance books, Reader's Digest Condensed. Ah, here's a classic. *Anna Karenina.* I never could finish that. (*Tries to pull it out.*)

MAN. (*Delighted.*) I remember it. It's about trains.

JANE. (*As SHE pulls it out, a whole section comes with it but they are just cardboard spines of books glued together.*) What a crock. They aren't real books. It's just for show.

MAN. Surface culture.

JANE. (*Puts cardboard row of books back.*) Like those TV ads for three record albums that have "all the music you'll ever need." And here's all the movies you'll ever need on tape.

MAN. Here it is. "Amnesia." (*Reads some from book.*)

JANE. What's it say?

MAN. I have "functional amnesia." That's what it says. (*Shows her the book.*)

JANE. "Functional amnesia."

MAN. (*Takes book back.*) There is nothing to do for it but wait and it will clear up.

JANE. (*Crosses C.*) How long? An hour? A month? A lifetime?

MAN. It just says wait. (*As HE puts book back.*) At least I am functional.

JANE. (*Crosses to window and looks out.*) And you may have to function very soon. We can't just loaf. I have a job to do. There is danger here. Probably.

MAN. Possibly.

JANE. Definitely.

MAN. (*Goes to sofa.*) I have to stay and help. I have nowhere to go. (*Sits.*)

JANE. And maybe you do belong here. (*Sits by him.*)

MAN. But what if you're the Master Criminal and you're only using me?

JANE. It's possible but then I'd know it and you wouldn't.

MAN. (*Sits.*) I'll have to think that one over.

JANE. (*Sits beside him.*) Then we best continue to be married.

MAN. (*As HE leans in.*) Good.

JANE. Wait. Maybe you're already married.

MAN. I don't think so. (*Holds up left hand.*) No wedding ring.

JANE. Maybe that was stolen with your wallet.

MAN. No white marks where a ring was on third finger left hand. I am a bachelor. I am available. Are you married?

JANE. No.

MAN. Do you have an arrangement?

JANE. If you mean am I seeing someone, yes.

MAN. Oh.

JANE. Several someones in fact. I am quite popular.

MAN. I'm sure I am, too. Now, if anyone else shows up how do we know he's telling the truth?

JANE. We mustn't believe anyone. Not even— (*Points up to ceiling.*)

MAN. I'm not a very religious man, but—

JANE. No, not him. You know. (*Points again.*)

MAN. Oh, you mean—? (*Points up.*)

(*THEY nod in unison as VERLA comes downstairs carrying a light bulb.*)

MAN and JANE. (*Together.*) Verla.

VERLA. Yes. (*Surprised, THEY put hands down.*) What's wrong?

MAN. I thought there was a leak in the ceiling.

JANE. Yes, I felt a drop of water.

VERLA. (*Comes down and puts hand out.*) Don't feel none. Don't see none. No plumber tonight anyways. Daniel is busy. His Minnie is havin' her fourth.

MAN. Baby?

VERLA. Litter. Minnie is a cat.

JANE. (*Mops brow.*) It's sweat, that's all. We were exercising. (*Puts arms up and then down while sitting.*)

VERLA. (*Suspicious.*) Yeah?

MAN. (*Same gestures as Jane.*) Sit down aerobics. It's the latest thing.

(*THEY continue to stretch up and down as HE counts.*)

MAN. One, two—

VERLA. I came down for a light bulb. This one in Daffodil is dead.

MAN. Daffodil?

VERLA. All the rooms is named for flowers. This here rattles when you shake it. (*Shakes it by his ear.*)

MAN. Sure does rattle.

VERLA. Dead as my Calvin. You keep exercisin' and I'll get a bulb. (*Goes U.C.*)

JANE. (*Rises and goes to her as MAN keeps exercising.*) Verla.

VERLA. Yeah.

JANE. Is your present husband's name Perkins or did you keep your maiden name?

VERLA. His name's Perkins. Gotta keep changin' my name with each marriage so's I get new towels with new initials on them. I got closets full of terry cloth. (*Exits down hall.*)

MAN. (*As HE unconsciously continues the arm exercises and SHE rushes to the desk.*) What was all that about?

JANE. I want to see if Verla is for real.

MAN. How can you prove it?

JANE. (*Looking in phone book.*) I wanted to get her last name to see if she's in the phone book.

MAN. Smart.

JANE. Put your arms down. You look like a robot.

MAN. (*Does so.*) Say, that really gets the shoulders.

JANE. (*Moves D.C.*) Aha! There is not one Perkins in this book.

MAN. (*Goes to her.*) Maybe Verla commutes.

JANE. From where?

MAN. How do I know from where? I don't even know from where I am.

JANE. Sorry.

VERLA. (*Enters with 25 watt light bulb.*) I'm puttin' in a 25 watt. Saves money. Them city folks always leave lights on. (*Starts to go upstairs.*)

JANE. Verla, we ought to have a phone number for you in case of an emergency.

VERLA. Right you are. (*Goes to desk.*) I'll write it out here.

MAN. (*Looks to Jane.*) She'll write it out.

JANE. I guess I could just look in the book.

VERLA. Book wouldn't do no good.

JANE. Why not?

VERLA. Unlisted. Don't want no strangers callin' me up. Don't like all that heavy breathin'

(*Starts up the stairs and turns back.*) Unless I'm doin' it. (*Exits.*)

MAN. (*Sinks on sofa.*) So we've proved nothing.

JANE. (*Looks at what Verla wrote.*) I'm going to call this number. (*Dials.*)

MAN. And if Verla answers then Verla isn't Verla?

JANE. Not our Verla anyway.

MAN. When my memory comes back I hope I'm not married to her.

JANE. I think she would have mentioned it. (*Listens.*) Oh, drat! (*Hangs up.*)

MAN. Busy signal?

JANE. (*Crosses C.*) Answering machine. She—or whoever—has an answering machine.

MAN. What's it say?

JANE. Short and curt. It said, "I am out!"

MAN. So Verla might really be Verla?

JANE. And you might be anyone at all.

MAN. (*Goes to her at C.*) Suppose I'm here to deliver the package? Where is it? Let's look. It must be somewhere. (*Goes D.L.*) Let's investigate. I have no memory of this place. I must get acclimated.

JANE. Acclimated. You do have a great vocabulary.

MAN. Thanks, but I'm not sure what acclimated means.

(*THEY exit D.L.*

As THEY exit, SYLVIA's face appears at the
window, SHE crosses down and opens door and
calls behind her.)

SYLVIA. No one's here.
DEXTER. (*Offstage.*) Then how did the lights
get on?
SYLVIA. I mean no one is here in this very
room. It's safe to come in.
DEXTER. (*Offstage.*) With the bags?
SYLVIA. We're tourists, aren't we? I'll carry
my own.
DEXTER. (*Offstage.*) Good.
SYLVIA. Then we'll look married.

(SYLVIA goes outside as MAN and JANE come in
hallway to below stairs.)

JANE. Now upstairs. (*As THEY start to go,*
SHE first.) And let's be sure the towels match the
face cloths.
MAN. No, the face rags.
JANE. Game room, bar, kitchen, what more do
we want?
MAN. (*As THEY disappear.*) A crook or a
mastermind or a Godfather—
JANE. But most of all a package.
MAN. Or an identity for me.

(DEXTER comes in followed by SYLVIA. THEY
both carry small overnight bags and SHE a
purse and a raincoat or topper.)

DEXTER. This is the damndest Bed and Breakfast. No one is here. Do we register or what? (*Puts suitcase down.*)

SYLVIA. How do I know? You're in charge. (*Puts bag down and coat over back of sofa. SHE takes a listening device from her purse or pocket. It is a very small square box resembling a radio. SHE walks around with it starting above the sofa.*)

DEXTER. We should have planned it better. The office—

SYLVIA. Shh!

DEXTER. What are you doing?

SYLVIA. (*Whispers.*) Don't say anything incriminating ...

DEXTER. You're right. Bugs.

SYLVIA. (*Crosses up to shelves still whispering.*) Keep up the act. We might be recorded.

DEXTER. (*Goes to her and whispers.*) I'm sure no one knows we're here.

SYLVIA. (*Looks on and in the desk.*) The department didn't send us on a wild goose chase.

DEXTER. What about the other departments? They're riddled with jealousy.

SYLVIA. You're right. This place could he crawling with agents. Trust no one.

DEXTER. Except you, of course, and myself.

SYLVIA. Room's clean. (*Puts device back in purse.*)

DEXTER. Looks spotless.

SYLVIA. Clean means no recording devices.

DEXTER. You're so colloquial.

SYLVIA. (*Has taken chair from C. of desk and is about to stand on it to look through books on top shelves.*) I know.

DEXTER. You're also conceited.

SYLVIA. (*Sees book before getting onto chair.*) Look at that. (*Pulls out cardboard set.*) A fake *Anna Karenina*.

DEXTER. What does she do in the new version, throw herself in front of a B-29?

(*SYLVIA climbs up on chair. DEXTER moves to C. of her.*)

SYLVIA. If the books are false, then maybe up here somewhere—

(*MAN and JANE have comes downstairs and watch.*)

MAN. (*Very politely.*) I beg your pardon.

(*DEXTER grabs SYLVIA as SHE gives a cry and almost falls dropping a book on the floor.*)

DEXTER. Hang on!

SYLVIA. I was just getting a book to read me to sleep.

MAN. (*Picks up book from floor.*) *The Bobsy Twins in Europe.* That should do it.

SYLVIA. Brings back my childhood.

DEXTER. (*After an awkward pause, takes book and hands it back to her.*) You may wonder what we're doing here.

MAN. It did cross my mind.

JANE. (*Crosses to them, the perfect hostess.*) How do you do. I am Jane—(*Looks to Man for help.*)

MAN. Roderman.

JANE. (*At same time.*) Lister. Yes, all three names. I come from the South.

DEXTER. I am Dexter Chandler and this is Sylvia Dutton.

SYLVIA. Chandler. Sylvia Dutton Chandler. We Southerners have to stick together, don't we?

JANE. And we do lose our accents, don't we?

(*THEY smile knowingly.*)

MAN. (*To Sylvia still standing on the chair.*) Why don't you come down and join us?

SYLVIA. (*As DEXTER helps her down.*) Yes, of course.

MAN. (*Crosses away below sofa.*) Other than lending a book, can we do anything else for you?

DEXTER. Is the manager about?

MAN. I am the manager.

DEXTER. I assumed you were both guests.

SYLVIA. Yes. (*To Jane.*) You said your name was Lister.

JANE. That's right.

SYLVIA. (*Crosses to L. of desk.*) But you are Roger Lenox.

DEXTER. The manager.

MAN. Yes—

JANE. (*Comes down.*) We're not married.

SYLVIA. How modern. I hope this place is not booked solid.

DEXTER. Jason Meadows at the office said this was such a perfect place for a weekend.

MAN. Jason Meadows?

DEXTER. (*Takes out wallet and hands large bill to Man.*) Since you're a bachelor then I know you understand how important it is to have a quiet room for the weekend. (*Nudges him.*)

MAN. (*Takes the bill.*) Of course.

JANE. We can accommodate them, can't we— Roger?

MAN. If you say so. Any friend of Jason Whatever—

DEXTER. Meadows. Jason Meadows. He sends lots of couples just like us.

SYLVIA. (*Moves in.*) Not tonight, I hope.

MAN. The place is yours.

SYLVIA. (*Gets coat from back of sofa and moves U.C.*) Perhaps we should go and unpack.

MAN. (*Picks up both suitcases.*) I'll help you with your bags.

DEXTER. (*Takes them from him and goes below Sylvia to U.C.*) Nonsense, old man. No bellboys in a B and B, eh?

JANE. (*Takes raincoat from Sylvia.*) Here, let me hang this up for you.

SYLVIA. Thanks very much.

JANE. (*Crosses below them to closet and hangs up coat.*) We have a guest bathroom over there.

MAN. (*Goes D.L.*) In case you're trapped in the bar then you don't have to go all the way upstairs. (*Opens door.*) Bar is through here.

DEXTER. (*Steps down.*) Good.

SYLVIA. Which room is ours?

MAN. Yes, which?

JANE. Daffodil.

MAN. Yes, the one called Daffodil.

JANE. You take them up, Roger.

MAN. No, you do it. Daffodil? It's the yellow room. You're so good at knowing which room will suit which people. (*To others.*) It's a knack she has.

SYLVIA. (*As SHE and JANE go upstairs.*) It's so charming here. You must have a decorator's eye.

JANE. (*With a look back at Man.*) It's just another knack I have.

DEXTER. (*Goes to foot of stairs and turns back.*) I'll meet you in the bar there and we can trade stories about Jason. He's such a joker, isn't he? (*HE goes upstairs.*)

MAN. (*Left alone.*) But the joke's on me.

VERLA. (*Offstage upstairs.*) You people guests?

DEXTER. (*Offstage.*) Yes.

JANE. (*Offstage.*) They're in here, the Daffodil room.

VERLA. (*Offstage.*) Towels is in the bathroom but they don't match. It's off-season. (*Comes downstairs.*)

SYLVIA. (*Offstage.*) I'm sure it's charming.

VERLA. (*To Man.*) I thought you was honeymoonin'. That usually means alone.

MAN. (*Goes to her.*) You know, Verla, a couple of extra bucks helps.

VERLA. I better check the larder for breakfast fixin's.

MAN. Do you cook, too?

VERLA. For money, yes. For free, no. But you know, Milton, a couple of extra bucks helps. (*Laughs as SHE goes down hallway.*)

MAN. (*Looks after her and then crosses down.*) Maybe she's right and I am Milton Roderman. No, Roger Lenox. Why don't people just say, "Hi, Man" or "Hello, darling," something simple like that?

(*Front door opens and KITTY is there. SHE is probably in her thirties, pretty in a slightly overdone way but very friendly and easy going. SHE carries an overnight case and a purse.*)

KITTY. Hi, darling. (*Puts her case down, throws her purse on the sofa and descends on Man with arms open wide.*)

MAN. Now that's what I mean. Hello.

KITTY. (*After giving him a huge kiss.*) I bet you're surprised.

MAN. You win your bet.

KITTY. I didn't think you'd be open but I took a chance and saw the lights on and here I am.

MAN. Yes, you certainly are here.

KITTY. Why did you stay open, Willy?

MAN. Willy?

KITTY. Geez, I forgot. Sorry. Willis. I know you hate Willy.

MAN. I'm not that fond of Willis either. Call me by my last name.

KITTY. No, that sounds silly.

MAN. Oh, go on.

KITTY. All right, Buttram.

MAN. You're right, it does sound silly.

KITTY. (*Goes to foot of stairs and glances up them.*) You're not full, are you?

MAN. It's getting closer by the minute.

KITTY. (*Comes down as HE crosses below sofa.*) First time you've stayed open for the foliage season. Why aren't you in Lauderdale by now?

MAN. Florida?

KITTY. Yeah.

MAN. I rented that place out for another month so here I am.

KITTY. (*Sits on bench and leans back.*) Naughty boy. Why didn't you tell me last time I was here.

MAN. That was so long ago. (*Goes to her.*) Wasn't it?

KITTY. Couple of weeks. Yeah, mid-July it was. I was between the Catskills and Maine. I tell my agent not to book me two nights in a row with travelling in between. My voice isn't as young as it used to be.

MAN. *(Sits by her.)* The rest of you looks good though.

KITTY. You're sweet. *(Kisses his cheek.)*

MAN. Everything look the same to you here?

KITTY. *(Looks around.)* Sure.

MAN. Even me? I look the same?

KITTY. Now you mention it—no.

MAN. Oh?

KITTY. You had a haircut.

MAN. You noticed.

KITTY. *(Rises suddenly.)* Paul! I'm forgetting Paul!

MAN. I'm Willie—Willis Buttram.

KITTY. Not you, Paul in the car. *(Goes to door.)* I told him to wait and I'd see if you were open.

MAN. The more the merrier.

KITTY. *(Opens door and calls.)* Paul, come on in. It's OK. *(Turns back to Man.)* I hope we can have separate rooms. We're not—you know.

MAN. I know.

KITTY. I knew you'd know.

MAN. *(Rises and goes C.)* You and I weren't—I mean, we didn't—did we?

KITTY. If we had, you'd remember it.

MAN. I'm sure I would.

KITTY. Not that I didn't try.

MAN. And I fought you off? I don't believe it.

KITTY. I might try again.

(PAUL comes running in the open door and goes below Kitty. HE is healthy, handsome, and hearty. HE is dressed in a sweat suit and carries a backpack. There is a sweat band on his head.)

PAUL. *(Goes right up to Man and shakes his hand heartily.)* Hi, there. You must be Willis Buttram.

MAN. Yes, I must be.

PAUL. Kitty here sure was surprised you're open.

MAN. So she said.

PAUL. I'm Paul Miles. I run.

MAN. I guessed that.

PAUL. And my name is Miles. Funny, huh?

MAN. Hilarious.

KITTY. I picked Paul up.

MAN. Really?

PAUL. Yeah. *(Puts his backpack on the sofa.)* I work in a health spa but I'm on vacation so I'm running through New England. *(Laughs.)* Hey, I don't mean non-stop. I walk some of the time, too. I was looking for a place to bed down but it's a helluva long way between villages up here.

KITTY. *(Sits on the sofa.)* I saw him doing push-ups by the side of the road. I couldn't just leave him there, could I?

MAN. *(Sits on the C. arm of the sofa.)* No way. He could have hurt his back pushing up like that.

PAUL. No, not me. Strong as an ox.

KITTY. And he looked so trustworthy.

PAUL. (*Smiles.*) Yeah.

KITTY. And he is so handsome.

PAUL. (*An even bigger smile.*) Yeah!

KITTY. So I asked him if he wanted a lift to the next town.

PAUL. (*Crosses C.*) And she suddenly swerves off the highway and I thought, "Whoa, Boy! This gal's up to something." It's happened to me before.

MAN. I can see why.

PAUL. (*Smiles.*) I guess you can.

KITTY. I wanted to swing by in case you were open.

PAUL. And you are, Willis, old man. (*Slaps him on the back.*) This sure is my lucky day.

KITTY. (*Rises and picks up her suitcase and purse.*) So which rooms are free?

MAN. (*Takes her suitcase.*) Just go on upstairs. There's another couple up there and a single girl. Jane. She'll take care of you.

PAUL. (*Gets his backpack.*) Great.

KITTY. Who is Jane, you little devil?

MAN. (*Gives her suitcase to Paul.*) Just a girl who's helping out.

PAUL. No problem, man. If she sees me I'll just cut down on the old charm. (*HE bounds upstairs.*)

KITTY. (*Goes to the foot of the stairs and turns back. SHE is suddenly more serious.*) I thought it was good to have him for a shield. Clever, huh?

MAN. Brilliant.

KITTY. You haven't bugged this place, have you?

MAN. No bugs. Just been sprayed.

KITTY. (*Laughs.*) That's cute.

PAUL. (*Offstage.*) Kitty, get a move on.

KITTY. (*Calls.*) Coming. (*To Man.*) We'll plan things out later. (*Goes upstairs.*)

MAN. (*Calls after her.*) What things?

KITTY. (*Offstage.*) Later.

MAN. Why not now? (*Comes back into room.*) What's this place like when it's open? (*PHONE rings.*) This is all I need, another threat to break my fingers one by one. (*JANE's recording comes on and during it HE speaks.*) Oh hell, I was hoping for a cancellation.

(*After JANE's voice stops, the VOICE from before comes on sounding even more ominous.*)

VOICE. Guess who?

MAN. I give up.

VOICE. You know who. My messenger is there by now so no tricks or the hills will be alive with the sound of breaking bones. Get me?

MAN. I get you.

VOICE. I knew you would. So the money is mine and you get the plates.

MAN. Plates? What plates?

VOICE. And I mean tonight. (*Clicks off.*)

MAN. (*Talking to the machine.*) What plates? China? TV dinner? Verla's upper teeth? What?

SYLVIA. (*Comes downstairs.*) Roger, darling.

(MAN continues staring at phone.)

SYLVIA. Roger.

MAN. That's me. Yes.

SYLVIA. Daffodil is too dark.

MAN. I beg your pardon.

SYLVIA. The room we're in, Daffodil. It's too dark.

MAN. *(Crosses L. of desk down to bench.)* Put on the light.

SYLVIA. The bulb is 25 watts. I exchanged it with the one in Marigold, the room next door.

MAN. Fine. Do whatever you like.

SYLVIA. *(Moves to him.)* I'm glad we're alone.

MAN. *(Uneasy.)* Are you?

SYLVIA. *(Whispers.)* You know why.

MAN. *(Goes below her to sofa.)* Wouldn't you rather be alone with macho Paul Miles? He's the jogger upstairs.

SYLVIA. No, you. We must—

VERLA. *(Offstage in the bar.)* Hello. Where are you, in the bar?

SYLVIA. Not now. *(Rushes to stairs.)* We'll make plans later.

MAN. When?

SYLVIA. *(As SHE runs upstairs.)* Later, in the bar.

MAN. It will be like the briefing room at the Pentagon.

VERLA. *(Comes in.)* Mice!

MAN. What?

VERLA. Mice got into the Honey Bunches of Oats.

MAN. What are you talking about?

VERLA. Honey Bunches of Oats. It's a cereal.

MAN. I never go beyond Wheaties, the Breakfast of Champions.

VERLA. What'll happen in the morning?

MAN. (*Sits on C. sofa arm.*) I'm worried about what will happen tonight.

VERLA. (*Crosses in.*) I better get some of that stuff city folks go for. You know, it has hay and straw and fruit poppin' and cracklin'.

MAN. All we need is toast and coffee.

VERLA. Nonsense. Store's closed, of course, but, bein' the sheriff, I got a passkey.

MAN. Wait till the morning.

VERLA. Nope. (*Goes to him and whispers.*) Say, when this place quiets down later we gotta have a meetin' and—

MAN. Plan things out?

VERLA. You got it. (*Slaps his back and crosses U.C.*) By then I'll be on overtime. (*Exits down hallways.*)

MAN. (*Rises and goes above desk.*) I give up. I'm calling the F.B.I., the C.I.A., the I.R.S., I don't care who the hell who.

JANE. (*Comes downstairs with suitcase just as HE picks up the phone.*) Don't! Don't phone anyone.

MAN. But that person called again and he's handing over the plates.

JANE. What plates?

MAN. How the hell do I know but if he isn't paid for them the hills will be alive with the sound of breaking bones. Mine. (*Picks up phone.*) I am going to call for help.

JANE. You've got me to help.

MAN. (*Puts phone down, starts getting frantic.*) Jane, you are marvelous. (*Goes to her.*) You are the kind of stranger I always wanted to meet across a crowded room but this is no enchanted evening.

JANE. I know it's getting out of hand but—

MAN. Besides, you are leaving.

JANE. I wouldn't leave you in the middle of all this.

MAN. Then why are you carrying a suitcase?

JANE. I found it in the Hydrangea room.

MAN. Do you think the plates are in there?

JANE. (*Puts the case on the bench facing C. with him behind her.*) Who knows? It's locked.

MAN. (*Crosses down.*) Where's a sledge hammer?

JANE. Don't be so macho. (*Leans across to desk.*) All we need is—ah, here we are. (*Holds up a paper clip which SHE bends straight.*)

MAN. What good is that?

JANE. (*As SHE attacks locks on case.*) It's replaced hair pins for picking locks.

MAN. Did you get trained in this?

JANE. Sure. "Safes and Locks 103." In the course it comes right between "Bomb Detonation" and "Target Practice During Freefall." (*Opens lock.*) There we are. (*Paper clip down on desk.*)

MAN. You continue to amaze me.

JANE. (*Goes L. of desk.*) Well, open it.

MAN. I hope it's plates. (*Opens it.*) Oh, hell.

JANE. What?

MAN. It's only money.

JANE. You do mean money, don't you, like in cash?

MAN. (*Turns suitcase front and it is full of wrapped packages of bills.*) Look!

JANE. It's Fort Knox.

MAN. I'm not expected to give this away, am I?

JANE. It's obviously part of the plot. It's to pay for the plates. It's not yours.

MAN. It's mine now.

JANE. How can it be yours when you don't know who you are?

MAN. It's going to belong to one of me, either Jack Lister, Roger Lenox, Milton Roderman or Willis Buttram.

JANE. I don't know that one.

MAN. That's what the latest couple call me.

JANE. (*Closes suitcase and goes C. with it.*) What we have to do is wait and see whoever comes out asking for the money and then we'll see what plates are so valuable.

MAN. (*Goes C. and his hands go on suitcase, too.*) And give this away?

JANE. Yes.

MAN. I suppose this must be illegal money?

JANE. A suitcase full of cash does not smack of a Girl Scout cookie sale.

MAN. What'll we do if someone comes?

JANE. They won't.

(KNOCK on door.)

MAN. They have.
JANE. *(Grabs the suitcase from him.)* The money, quick.
MAN. Where?
JANE. *(To closet.)* In here.
MAN. *(As JANE puts suitcase in closet.)* You, too. *(Pushes her in, closes door and starts for front door.)*
JANE. *(Opens door.)* Why me?
MAN. Guard the cash. Who knows who this is? It could be anyone from Heidi to the Bride of Frankenstein. *(Closes door and starts again for front door.)*

(Door opens and WILMA CHANDLER comes in at full tilt. SHE is a young middle age and dressed expensively.)

WILMA. *(Drops her overnight bag by the door.)* Leonard!
MAN. Me?
WILMA. *(Descends on him.)* Darling! It's been too long. *(Kisses him as closet door opens and JANE looks out. MAN waves frantically to her as:)*

CURTAIN

ACT II

Scene 1

Repeat back two speeches with WILMA saying:

WILMA. Leonard!
MAN. Me?
WILMA. (*Descends on him.*) Darling! It's been too long.

(WILMA kisses him as closet door opens and JANE looks out. MAN waves frantically to close the door and SHE does. WILMA breaks the kiss and looks around surprised.)

WILMA. Oh, no, we're alone.
MAN. More or less.
WILMA. I was sure he would be here.
MAN. Leonard?
WILMA. No. You're Leonard, aren't you?
MAN. Probably.
WILMA. (*Takes topcoat U.L. assuming it is the closet.*) I do apologize. Forgive me.
MAN. (*Closes front door.*) I rather enjoyed it.
WILMA. I know he is here so I wanted to make a good entrance.
MAN. It was quite spectacular.
WILMA. (*Opens door.*) This is a bathroom.

MAN. Yes, for guests.

WILMA. How convenient.

MAN. Closet is there.

WILMA. (*Goes to it.*) You see, I have every reason to believe Dexter Chandler is here and not alone.

MAN. His wife is here.

WILMA. Ha!

MAN. (*As SHE is about to open closet door, HE remembers Jane and crosses up to R. of sofa.*) Not in there!

WILMA. (*Opens door and JANE is standing there and takes the coat before WILMA realizes it and WILMA closes the door and goes C.*) I knew he would be here and—(*Freezes.*) There is a woman in that closet.

MAN. (*Points.*) There?

WILMA. Yes. (*Opens door and JANE is hanging up her coat.*) How do you do. I am Wilma Chandler.

JANE. And I am Jane Ridgely. (*Pause.*) It's all right. You don't need a coat check.

WILMA. (*Confused.*) Thank you. (*Closes the door and crosses C.*) Does she stay in there all the time?

MAN. (*Laughs.*) No. When you opened the front door the wind blew that one shut. (*Goes to closet.*) She'd come out but the handle sticks.

WILMA. (*Unconvinced.*) I see.

MAN. (*Opens closet door, to Jane.*) Come in and join us.

JANE. Thank you.

MAN. Door handle OK?

JANE. *(Looks at it.)* The handle?

MAN. Those squirts of three-in-one oil did the trick, eh?

JANE. *(To Wilma as MAN closes closet door.)* He's so handy around the house.

WILMA. I'm afraid I rather surprised Leonard.

JANE. Who?

MAN. Me? I'm Leonard.

JANE. Of course.

WILMA. Dexter is here, isn't he?

JANE. Dexter Chandler?

WILMA. Or is he under an assumed name?

MAN. *(Crosses below sofa.)* No, no, Dexter Chandler is it.

WILMA. *(Goes to him.)* And Sylvia Dutton?

MAN. Yes, Sylvia. That's his—no, you're his—oh, dear.

WILMA. I am his wife and she is his secretary.

JANE. *(Crosses down.)* Then it's a working tax deductible weekend.

WILMA. I learned of this place and you, Leonard, from Dexter's former secretary. She was demoted to the typing pool after she refused weekends like this.

JANE. And you are here to make a scene?

WILMA. I want to show him how it feels to have a spouse cheat on you. That's why I kissed you, Leonard. *(Goes right up to him.)* We are going to have an affair.

MAN. I hardly know you.

JANE. You only just met.

WILMA. I want Dexter to assume we are lovers. Won't that be fun?

MAN. Sounds better than Scrabble.

WILMA. (*Goes to Jane.*) What about you? Are you wife, mistress or do you only spend time hiding in Leonard's closet?

JANE. I'm just an old school chum.

MAN. That secretary of your husband's, the ex one—the secretary not your husband—did she mention my last name?

WILMA. Yes, when she gave me the address. Mulwray, isn't it?

MAN. Mulwray. Leonard Mulwray.

JANE. Yes, that's right.

WILMA. You're not booked solid, I hope.

MAN. Business is booming. (*Gets her bag from D.R.*) Let me show you to a room.

WILMA. I'll freshen up first.

MAN. (*Alarmed.*) First?

WILMA. (*To Jane.*) Which room is mine?

JANE. Coreopsis.

MAN. Sounds invigorating. doesn't it?

WILMA. (*To Man.*) Where will I find you later?

MAN. (*Goes above sofa.*) In the bar. It's through there.

WILMA. I'll be down in five minutes. (*To Jane.*) You won't mind us being real cozy in front of Dexter, will you, dear?

JANE. (*With a smile to Man.*) Sounds better than Scrabble.

KITTY. (*Calls from upstairs.*) Hey, sweetie, you downstairs?

WILMA. Sweetie?

JANE. (*Calls upstairs.*) We are down here, yes.

WILMA. It's that secretary. (*To Man.*) Kiss me. No, wait. I want Dexter to find us first. (*Grabs her suitcase and hides in closet.*) Get rid of her. (*Closes door as MAN breaks L. of sofa and Jane to below bench.*)

JANE. (*After their crosses.*) Do you feel like Leonard Mulwray?

MAN. Not at all.

KITTY. (*Comes downstairs carrying the 25 watt light bulb.*) There you are. I'm having trouble seeing. This light bulb is only 25 watts.

MAN. You must be in the Marigold room.

KITTY. Yeah.

MAN. (*Goes to her.*) Let me get you a higher wattage.

KITTY. Thanks. (*Goes to Jane.*) Or I'll be putting mascara on my lips. (*Laughs.*)

MAN. (*Starts for kitchen, turns back to Jane as HE realizes HE doesn't know where extra bulbs would be.*) Now where do you suppose I put those extra light bulbs?

JANE. The kitchen has a store room, doesn't it?

MAN. Does it?

JANE. Of course. They always do.

MAN. Of course. (*Exits down hallway.*)

JANE. Leonard is so nervous.

KITTY, Leonard?

JANE. Did I say Leonard?

KITTY. Yes, you did.

JANE. I meant Willis. His full name is Willis Leonard.

KITTY. Buttram.

JANE. (*Sits on bench.*) Willis Leonard Buttram. You got it.

KITTY. (*Sits beside Jane.*) I'm really Katherine Jean Carson, but when I entered into show business I went to Kitty and then Kit. Kit Carson. Get it? People know it's familiar.

JANE. That's cute. And you play nightclubs and the reps and such?

KITTY. Yeah, only in musicals though.

JANE. I bet you're good.

KITTY. Yeah, I got my reviews but they're in the car.

JANE. Musicals like *Brigadoon* and *My Fair Lady* and *Carousel*?

KITTY. All of them, every single one.

JANE. I'd love to see you in *Brigadoon* I bet you stopped the show singing "When I Marry Mr. Snow."

KITTY. Every single night and twice on matinee days.

JANE. Interesting.

MAN. (*Comes back in with new light bulb.*) Here we are, one hundred good watts.

KITTY. (*Gets the bulb but holds onto other one.*) Gee, thanks. I'll just get rid of this.

JANE. It's all right, I'll—

KITTY. (*Goes to stairs.*) I know this place is Bed and Breakfast and not Bed and Noshes, but is there any possibility of a sandwich or something? I'm starved.

JANE. I'm sure we can rustle something up.

KITTY. I'm not fussy. Anything on a plate. (*Exits.*)

JANE and MAN. Plate?

MAN. (*Crosses down.*) That word again.

JANE. (*Goes to him.*) She's a fake. I caught her in a lie.

MAN. How?

JANE. She said she sang "When I Marry Mr. Snow" in *Brigadoon.*

MAN. So?

JANE. It's from *Carousel.*

MAN. You're right. And she did ask for a plate.

JANE. *The* plate?

MAN. Why is it so valuable?

JANE. Shh!

MAN. Why? What?

JANE. (*Points to closet.*) Doors have ears.

MAN. I forgot. (*Goes to closet, opens door and WILMA is there bent over listening. SHE straightens up.*)

MAN. You can come out now.

WILMA. I was just tying my shoelaces.

JANE. But those shoes don't have laces.

WILMA. So that's why they're so loose. (*Comes out with the money suitcase.*) Is the coast clear?

MAN. Off we go to the Coreopsis room. (*Frantic look to Jane.*)

JANE. Turn left and down the hall.

MAN. Of course. (*Takes bag from Wilma, crosses below her to stairs.*) Just follow me.

JANE. Leonard. (*HE keeps going.*) Leonard. Hey, you!

MAN. Me?

JANE. Yes. You have the wrong suitcase.

MAN. I do? (*Looks down and realizes it.*) Oh, my God!! Wrong suitcase. (*Leaves the money one above the sofa and gets Wilma's from the closet during the following.*)

WILMA. I picked up the wrong one. Silly me.

JANE. Yes, silly you.

WILMA. Wouldn't it have been funny if I got to the room and nothing would fit.

MAN. Maybe it's one size fits all. (*Closes closet door.*)

WILMA. If we bump into my husband just kiss me and carry me across the threshold.

MAN. I'll try.

WILMA. (*Goes upstairs followed by MAN.*) And then back to the bar for a drink and a nibble, just something on a plate.

MAN. (*Exits after a look at Jane.*) Plate?

JANE. (*To herself.*) *Just* a plate, huh? (*Gets the suitcase, opens it on the sofa and looks at the money.*) Thousands. So crisp. So fresh. (*Picks out a pack.*) Look at this! I don't believe it! Yes, I do! (*Laughs and kisses the pack.*) Oh, bless you. Now we'll solve it. (*Closes suitcase and returns it to*

closet.) You are my trap. All I have to do is spring
it.

*(PAUL has come downstairs and to behind her
    before SHE closes the door. HE is constantly
    running in place.)*

PAUL. Not practical.

JANE. You scared me. *(Closes door.)*

PAUL. Running shoes. They're quiet.

JANE. What's not practical?

PAUL. Suitcase like that. Backpack, that's the
only way to go.

JANE. I guess it's too hard to jog with a heavy
suitcase.

PAUL. *(Jogs below desk.)* For the average guy,
yes. Me? It would slow me down but, you know, I
could handle it.

JANE. I'm sure you could handle anything.

PAUL. *(Smiles.)* Yeah.

JANE. Everything all right, your room and
all?

PAUL. If I could see it.

JANE. Pardon me?

PAUL. That's a joke. The bulb was burnt out
and Kitty gave me one but it's only 25 watts.

JANE. We have others.

PAUL. *(Jogs to below sofa.)* I'll need bright
light so I can check myself in the mirror. Want to
be sure the old face is still a classic.

JANE. You belong on Mount Rushmore.

PAUL. *(Pleased, but doesn't get it.)* Yeah?

JANE. (*Goes to him.*) If we're going to have a little chat, do you think you could stop bobbing?

PAUL. Huh?

JANE. You look like a drunken metronome.

PAUL. (*Stops.*) Sure but just for a minute. Gotta keep in trim.

JANE. That's better. When you're still you do look awfully familiar.

PAUL. Some TV star probably. I'm always asked for my autograph.

JANE. (*Sits on sofa.*) I'm sure I've seen you before somewhere.

PAUL. That's impossible.

JANE. Why?

PAUL. If you'd seen me before you wouldn't forget it. This is a face one remembers.

JANE. Yes.

PAUL. The body, too. It's not that I'm conceited—

JANE. No, not at all.

PAUL. It's just that it happens to be the truth.

JANE. I'll certainly see that you get a very bright bulb.

PAUL. Thanks. (*Opens front door and starts bobbing again.*) Now off for a short run.

JANE. It's night. There might be bears out there.

PAUL. So? (*Makes boxer hits.*) Any bear had better watch out. Besides, I left some home-made Trail Mix in the car. I need that energy fix.

JANE. (*A new attack to trap him.*) That sure was lucky Kitty Carson picked you up or we wouldn't have met.

PAUL. Yeah, she's a great gal. She tell you she's a singer?

JANE. She mentioned it. Did you ever see her in *Carousel*?

PAUL. (*Laughs.*) She wouldn't be any good in legit. She's great in a club, though.

JANE. I thought you just met.

PAUL. Oh, yeah. But she told me how great she is. (*Anxious to leave.*) I gotta go.

JANE. (*Gets up.*) Glad you're here.

PAUL. Yeah. I was tryin' to hitch a ride for a good half hour before Kitty came along. Usually have no trouble, not with this face and body but they were all local cars. When I saw Kitty's Subaru I knew I'd lucked out.

JANE. How?

PAUL. You can always tell with an out of state license plate. (*Goes out leaving the door open.*)

JANE. (*Goes to door.*) Plate?

PAUL. (*Offstage.*) Yeah, Washington. District of, not state of.

JANE. (*Closes door.*) Plate. Plate, Always plate.

MAN. (*Comes downstairs.*) Jane.

JANE. Yes, whatever your name is.

MAN. (*Goes below sofa.*) What'll we do? Now we have a jealous wife on top of everything else.

JANE. And there's something wrong with that macho jogger.

MAN. Is there? I'm glad. I was getting jealous.

JANE. He got messed up on his story about Kitty. He's known her before. And he talked about plates. License plates.

MAN. You're the investigator. (*Sits.*) So investigate.

JANE. (*Sits.*) I'm thinking.

MAN. Let's go back to being man and wife.

JANE. And have me married to a husband without a name?

MAN. Take your choice; Leonard Mulwray, Willis Buttram, Roger Lenox—

JANE. Milton Roderman—

MAN. And don't forget Jack Lister. He's my favorite.

JANE. I'm glad.

(*THEY almost kiss as DEXTER and SYLVIA come downstairs.*)

SYLVIA. Sorry, but I hope we are interrupting something.

JANE. (*As THEY both get up.*) Another minute and you might have.

DEXTER. I love to see a happy marriage.

MAN. (*Crosses below Jane to C.*) I'm sure yours is just as happy.

SYLVIA. Come along, Dexter. (*To others.*) We thought we'd have a drink—

DEXTER. Or two—

SYLVIA. Before we turn in.

(THEY are at bar door.)

DEXTER. *(Turns.)* A drink and just—
JANE. I know, something on a plate.
DEXTER. You got it. *(Exits.)*
MAN. *(Follows them to door.)* I don't trust them either. Let's listen in.
JANE. *(Joins him.)* They'll be at the bar and it's way across the room.

(THEY are both with their ears to the door.)

MAN. We might be able to catch a word or two.
WILMA. *(Has come downstairs and watches them.)* A glass to the wall works wonders.

(THEY straighten up and cross in a few steps.)

MAN. We didn't hear you.
WILMA. Obviously. *(Moves down.)* They're in there, are they?
JANE. Who do you mean?
WILMA. My husband and that woman.
MAN. Oh, them.
WILMA. This is the moment I have waited for. Come along, Leonard. *(Takes him by the arm below Jane and to the bar door.)*
MAN. No, I don't think you—
WILMA. You are my ace in the hole. Here we go. *(SHE wraps an arm around him.)* Look happy. We are lovers. *(Laughs gaily.)*
MAN. Jane, help—

WILMA. Laugh.

(HE does but weakly as THEY exit and WILMA raises her voice.)

WILMA. Leonard, darling—
JANE. Goodbye, young lovers.
KITTY. *(Comes downstairs carrying a lipstick as JANE still laughs.)* What's so funny?
JANE. It's a little complicated to explain.
KITTY. Do you have a Kleenex? I need to blot my lips.
JANE. In the bathroom there.
KITTY. It's a new color my accountant gave me. "Bookkeeper Red." *(Exits into bathroom.)*

(JANE starts for door D.L. when there is a SCREAM from the bar and WILMA hurtles out almost hitting Jane. SHE is followed by MAN.)

WILMA. No! No! It can't be!
MAN. What's wrong?
JANE. What happened?
WILMA. *(At C.)* That isn't his secretary. It's some other woman. Dexter is not only two-timing me, he is three-timing and who knows-how many-timing me.
JANE. *(Goes to her.)* Come upstairs with me and we'll have a nice woman-to-woman chat.
WILMA. It's too late. I am leaving. Where's my suitcase? *(Goes to closet.)*

MAN. (*Goes below bench.*) It's not in there, it's upstairs.

WILMA. (*Turns in closet.*) Oh, that's right.

DEXTER. (*Offstage in bar.*) Wilma, come back here!

WILMA. I can't speak to him. (*Closes herself in closet.*)

JANE. (*Crosses to closet.*) Wait, please—

MAN. There's going to be a murder.

DEXTER. (*Comes in.*) Where is she?

JANE. Who?

MAN. You must mean your wife.

DEXTER. Yes.

MAN. She was here a minute ago. She seems upset.

DEXTER. She doesn't understand about business weekends. (*Claps Man on the shoulder.*) Nothing to worry about. She'll recover. You know how it is, old man.

MAN. I wish I did.

DEXTER. (*Goes to stairs.*) It will all work out. Good night, Roger. (*Exits.*)

MAN. Good night, old man. (*Twirls around as OTHERS come in one after the other.*)

VERLA. (*From hallway.*) I got the breakfast stuff. Good night, Mr. Roderman. (*Goes back down hallway.*)

PAUL. (*Comes jogging in front door munching from small bag of his Trail Mix.*) Great stuff, this Trail Mix. Good night, Buttram. (*Runs upstairs.*)

SYLVIA. (*Comes in from bar pulling herself together.*) This is all rather embarrassing. (*Goes upstairs.*) Good night, Mr. Lenox.

KITTY. (*Comes out of bathroom.*) There, that's better. Good night, Willis. (*Goes upstairs.*)

WILMA. (*Comes out of closet.*) I am completely stressed out. (*Realizes suitcase in her hands is not hers.*) Oh, this is not mine. (*Puts it down.*) Good night. Leonard. (*Goes upstairs.*)

MAN. Is that all of them? Is there no one else?

JANE. (*Smiles.*) Good morning, Jack Lister. (*Laughs and HE doesn't.*)

CURTAIN

Scene 2

Later the same evening. PHONE rings. Same message from JANE comes on and during that the curtain opens. VERLA comes in from hallway and starts for it as JANE comes downstairs.

JANE. I've got it, Verla.

PAUL. (*Comes jogging in from outside.*) Phone's ringing.

MAN. (*Comes out of bathroom.*) I'm here.

JANE. (*Continued during above, SHE is R. of Verla.*) You run along.

VERLA. It might be for me. I'm the sheriff.

MAN. That's right.

JANE. *(To Paul.)* Then you run along.

PAUL. Might be for Kitty, her agent.

(ALL freeze as message comes on the machine. It is not the same voice, but a more cultured male one than before.)

VOICE. This is you-know-who.

MAN. Who knows who?

PAUL. Don't look at me.

JANE. Shh! *(JANE goes to Man above desk.)*

VOICE. It's imperative that you-know-which of-you calls you-know-who-I-am. There have been serious developments. I cannot say more till you call. Hurry! *(Clicks off.)*

MAN. *(After THEY all exchange a look.)* Who is you-know-which-of-you who is supposed to call you-know-who?

PAUL. *(Goes U.C.)* I got lost after the first you-know-who.

MAN. Is there a replay button?

JANE. The call must be for one of the others.

PAUL. I'll tell them. I have to brush my teeth anyway, keep these old dentures sparkling. *(Goes upstairs.)*

MAN. *(Goes below Jane to Verla.)* Verla, why are you still here?

VERLA. Breakfast.

MAN. Do you know what time it is?

VERLA. I'm makin' a real authentic Danish coffee ring.

JANE. What's wrong with Sara Lee?

VERLA. What's she know from Danish? She's American. (*Exits hallway.*)

MAN. I suppose Verla Perkins is an old Copenhagen name?

JANE. Like Victor Borge. (*Dials the phone.*)

MAN. What are you doing?

JANE. Phoning.

MAN. You mean you are you-know-who?

JANE. That was my boss. You go stand guard so no one hears.

MAN. (*Goes to window and looks out.*) This is getting even more confusing. You are you-know-who and I am I-don't-know-who.

JANE. (*Whispers into phone.*) Hello, this is— (*Looks around.*)—you-know-who.

MAN. (*Glances into closet.*) Here we go again.

JANE. (*Into phone.*) Oh, no ... when?... Yes, yes, I understand. I will.

MAN. (*At foot of stairs, whispers.*) Someone's stirring up there.

JANE. (*Into phone.*) What did he say before he died?

MAN. Died?

JANE. (*To Man.*) Shot.

MAN. (*Moves down to her.*) Why did I walk into this house? Why wasn't it a Holiday Inn?

JANE. (*Into phone.*) He said what? "The bagful of money buys the handful of money"?

MAN. The shot man said that?

JANE. (*To him.*) Then he died laughing.

MAN. (*Goes to foot of stairs.*) The punch line escapes me.

JANE. (*Into phone.*) No, I won't trust anyone here.

MAN. Someone is coming.

JANE. (*Into phone.*) I gotta go. (*Hangs up.*)

MAN. What's happened?

JANE. The man who kept leaving messages has been shot but he said, "The bagful of money buys a handful of money" before he died.

MAN. (*Looks in closet.*) Laughing. Great sense of humor. This suitcase of money is to buy the plates whatever they are?

JANE. You got it.

MAN. But who is the bad guy?

JANE. (*Glances upstairs.*) Whoever comes to the phone. The caller said for you-know-who to call.

MAN. God knows, I know that.

JANE. But the others don't know it was my boss so they'll think the message was for them.

MAN. Who is going to go to the phone?

JANE. The guilty one and right now. (*Closes door with them both inside.*)

(*WILMA comes downstairs and goes to the phone, picks it up, starts to dial and hears someone. SHE ducks into the bathroom as VERLA comes in from hallway and goes to phone and starts to dial. SHE hears someone and ducks into the barroom as KITTY comes downstairs, goes to phone and dials but hears someone, rushes about and ends up opening closet door and sees Jane and Man.)*

KITTY. Oh!

MAN. (*Smiling.*) Hi.

JANE. We're playing sardines and you've found us.

KITTY. Great. I love games.

(SHE goes in and closes door as SYLVIA and DEXTER come downstairs.)

SYLVIA. The coast is clear.

DEXTER. (*As THEY get to phone.*) I'll call the office.

WILMA. (*Comes out of bathroom.*) Caught you!

DEXTER. Wilma! I thought you left.

SYLVIA. What are you doing in that bathroom?

WILMA. I think that's rather personal. I'd rather know what you are doing here with him.

DEXTER. We're working.

WILMA. Together?

SYLVIA. Jealous?

WILMA. (*Goes R. of desk.*) Does the office know about this?

SYLVIA. (*At phone.*) That is who I am trying to call if you'll give me a minute.

WILMA. (*Goes to closet.*) While you're wasting your time I'm going to find out what is in that suitcase.

DEXTER. What suitcase?

WILMA. That one in the closet that no one seems to claim.

DEXTER. You think—?

WILMA. Precisely.

SYLVIA. You get it, Dexter.

WILMA. No way. What's in here is mine. (*Opens door and the THREE are huddled together.*)

KITTY. We're sardines.

MAN. You may think this is peculiar.

DEXTER. (*Crosses C.*) What the hell are you doing huddled in there?

JANE. Eavesdropping.

WILMA. I give up. (*Crosses to bench and sits.*)

KITTY. Is the game over? I'm getting claustrophobia.

JANE. Yes Out, out, out.

(*KITTY goes to R., of sofa, MAN above sofa, and JANE C., of sofa.*)

SYLVIA. I don't believe you two are married.

WILMA. They're not, are they?

SYLVIA. (*Sits chair C., of desk.*) Didn't she say they were?

KITTY. (*Sits sofa.*) Who cares?

DEXTER. Let's get this straight. (*To Jane.*) Are you married to Roger Lenox?

JANE. Definitely not.

KITTY. Who is Roger Lenox?

DEXTER. (*Points to Man.*) He is.

KITTY. No. He is Willis Buttram.

MAN. (*Crosses down to Wilma.*) She called me Leonard.

WILMA. I had to call him something.

JANE. I call him Jack Lister.

MAN. And Verla calls me Milton Roderman.

DEXTER. So who are you?

MAN. It doesn't matter who I am but you are all people who are leaving.

SYLVIA. (*Rises.*) But we—

MAN. Now! Out!

SYLVIA. (*Goes up to Dexter.*) I told you this wouldn't work.

DEXTER. It wasn't my idea.

SYLVIA. Who said we could work together without her?

WILMA. (*Rises. To Dexter.*) Without me you're nothing.

DEXTER. (*Goes to Wilma.*) Sylvia said it was time to change partners.

WILMA. (*To Sylvia.*) You're a second-string agent and always have been.

SYLVIA. (*Crosses down.*) I've been stuck in that office for years. I need some field work.

KITTY. You want to be a farmer?

JANE. (*Crosses C.*) Let's all calm down, shall we? It's obvious you're all undercover agents. You two are not married. Wilma is Dexter's ex-partner not his wife.

MAN. Why is no one who he should be?

JANE. (*Goes to him.*) Because they are all working for the government in one agency or another.

SYLVIA. (*Goes U.C.*) What if we are? What. about you two? (*To Man.*) He's so dumb he answers to any name you call him.

MAN. She's right.

DEXTER. (*Goes to stairs.*) We've all botched up the assignment. I suggest we cut our losses, go back to Washington, and say nothing of this to any superior. (*Starts up the stairs.*)

WILMA. (*As SHE and SYLVIA start for the stairs.*) That's the first time I've agreed with you this evening.

SYLVIA. (*Meets WILMA U.C.*) I really sympathize with you. How have you worked with him all these years?

WILMA. Simple. I have the brain power.

DEXTER. Now, Wilma. (*HE is off.*)

SYLVIA. (*To Wilma.*) We should be partners and ignore the male ego.

WILMA. (*As THEY disappear upstairs.*) That's like ignoring the atom bomb.

JANE. (*Turns to Kitty.*) As for you—

KITTY. (*Goes below sofa to U.C.*) I fell for that quiz about *Brigadoon*, didn't I?

JANE. You sure did.

KITTY. Stupid. I feel like a has been who never was.

MAN. Then I'm not Willis Buttram?

KITTY. Pity. Nice name, isn't it?

MAN. Are you with the CIA?

KITTY. One of those initialed agencies, yes.

JANE. Why don't you get your bag and pick up your health nut?

KITTY. Yeah. (*As SHE exits upstairs.*) I didn't do so well. Night club singer, ha! I shoulda said I was a test pilot for Boeing.

MAN. (*Left alone with Jane.*) Will you tell me what is going on?

JANE. (*Starts searching the room with MAN following her. First SHE looks out the window.*) They're all agents. They're all out of different departments.

MAN. What departments?

JANE. You have no idea of the jealousy in governmental agencies even though we're all after the same thing.

MAN. The plates?

JANE. (*Glances in bar.*) The plates.

MAN. Even Kitty is false?

JANE. Must be a newcomer. She didn't do enough research on her character.

MAN. That jogging macho stud?

JANE. (*Goes U.C., looks down hall and then to desk and goes through drawers.*) I'm not sure of him. And then we have Sheriff Verla Perkins.

MAN. (*Is C. of her.*) And there is one more you've overlooked.

JANE. Who?

MAN. Me.

JANE. No, I trust you.

MAN. Why? Maybe I am very good at inspiring trust. It may be my specialty.

JANE. I'll have to chance it.

MAN. What are you looking for? Don't tell me. The plates. What kind of plates can they be?

JANE. The clue lies in those dying words—
"the bagful of money buys a handful of money."
(*SHE is at shelves.*)

MAN. (*Brings suitcase to sofa.*) I bet they're in
the suitcase.

JANE. No, that money is to buy the plates.
(*Holds up one of the video tape boxes.*) Maybe this
will give us an idea.

MAN. What?

JANE. This video tape.

MAN. What is it?

JANE. *The Color of Money.*

MAN. You think that will help?

JANE. No, but it would be nice to see Paul
Newman and Tom Cruise again. (*Replaces tape.*)

MAN. (*Opens suitcase and reaches under
money.*) Look at all this. I've always wanted to
take a bath in money.

JANE. (*Goes to him.*) It's a crime to launder it.

MAN. Nothing here, just cash. Listen to me.
Just cash. Thousands of dollars. Look! (*Holds up
a wrapper.*)

JANE. That's a bagful of money all right.

MAN. You're not allowed to keep any, are you?

JANE. Not on your life.

MAN. Not even a tiny sample?

JANE. Wait a minute now. (*Runs back to
tapes.*) I've got it! I've got it! I am Jane Ridgely,
girl investigator, again.

MAN. What is it?

JANE. I know it! I know it! I am a genius! (*Takes out a tape box and out of it takes two metal printing plates about the size of a bill.*) Voila!

MAN. (*Crosses in.*) What are they?

JANE. (*Goes to him.*) Plates. Printing plates.

MAN. I can get those at any printing shop.

JANE. Not like these you can't. (*Examines them closely.*) Look at the work on them.

MAN. Is it good?

JANE. Brilliant. You can print a fortune with these.

MAN. They're not—? (*Turns to suitcase.*)

JANE. They sure are.

MAN. You mean—?

MAN. Counterfeit. (*Closes suitcase and goes to closet.*) This means one of those people upstairs brought this money here to buy the plates but he didn't know they were already here.

MAN. Why not!

JANE. The top man must have brought them here as a guest and hidden them. Then he sends his messenger up to hand them over and get the suitcase of money. That way the top man is never connected with the hand-over. (*Puts suitcase in closet.*)

MAN. But the messenger was killed first?

JANE. And gave us the clue about the handful of money.

MAN. What a mini-series this will make.

JANE. (*Crosses away below desk.*) Now let's do the expected.

MAN. What's that?

JANE. Gather all the suspects in this room.

MAN. And you'll solve it?

JANE. I have a trap. It only needs springing.

MAN. (*Goes to foot of stairs.*) I'm up for anything. (*Calls.*) Hello, up there! Come down. Everyone out of the pool. Let's go. Fun and games down here. (*Goes back to Jane.*) And me? What about me? Who am I?

JANE. That we might find out, too.

VERLA. (*Comes in from hallway.*) What's all the shoutin'. It'll flatten my coffee ring.

MAN. This is more important than coffee rings.

VERLA. (*Moves down.*) Even coffee rings with raisins and almonds?

MAN. Well—

SYLVIA. (*Comes downstairs followed by WILMA and goes below sofa.*) Go? Stay? Which do you want us to do?

WILMA. (*Goes below sofa and sits. SYLVIA sits also.*) After tonight, I may resign and go into aluminum siding.

DEXTER. (*Comes downstairs and goes above sofa.*) From this moment on I work alone like James Bond.

WILMA. He has sex appeal.

SYLVIA. And he always caught the bad guys.

KITTY. (*Comes downstairs.*) Do you want me, too?

JANE. You and Hercules up there.

KITTY. (*Goes R. of sofa.*) He's rubbing on liniment. He overdid it.

MAN. It seems everyone has overdone it tonight.

PAUL. (*Comes downstairs.*) I was up to eighty-three and aiming for one hundred push-ups.

SYLVIA. That won't work. We can smell the liniment.

PAUL. (*Goes to Kitty.*) You and your big mouth.

DEXTER. Why did you call us?

WILMA. We're all suspects and we're all in the living room, aren't we?

SYLVIA. She's going to solve the mystery.

JANE. (*Goes C.*) We all agree that no one here is who he says he is right?

MAN. Except you.

JANE. Except me. I *am* Jane Ridgely.

VERLA. And I am Verla, no doubt about that.

JANE. Verla, since you are the sheriff—

KITTY. That one is a sheriff?

VERLA. You're damned tootin.'

JANE. Verla, you better call Zeke Lundy at the State Troopers and get him up here.

VERLA. Oh, yeah, right away. (*Goes above desk to phone and MAN goes to the left of the desk.*)

PAUL. The State Troopers? This must be important.

JANE. (*As VERLA stands by phone.*) Go on, Verla, call.

VERLA. But it's the middle of the night.

JANE. (*Picks up the phone and hands it to her.*) Call him at home. Wake him up.

VERLA. I forget the number.

JANE. The phone book is right there.

VERLA. I can handle this I'm the sheriff. I—

MAN. Jane caught you, didn't she?

JANE. (*Puts the phone down.*) I sure did.

DEXTER. Caught her how?

MAN. I don't know. (*To Jane.*) How?

JANE. (*Moves away U.C.*) There is no Zeke Lundy. (*Turns to Verla.*) But you didn't know it, did you, Verla?

VERLA. (*Drops her country accent and also most of her character.*) So?

SYLVIA. Then who are you?

VERLA. (*Crosses C.*) I happen to outrank all of you at the agency.

WILMA. Which agency?

VERLA. (*Sits in chair C. of desk.*) That's for you to find out.

MAN. (*Moves in.*) So you're all good guys. Does no one wear a black hat?

DEXTER. What about —? (*Looks at Paul and THEY all turn to him.*)

PAUL. (*Crosses D.R.*) Hey. what's all this about? I'm just a normal guy who got picked up by the wrong broad.

KITTY. That's me.

JANE. I've got it.

MAN. What?

JANE. Paul, you stand up here. (*HE moves U.C.*) Dexter, you move in.

PAUL. What are you doing? What's this accomplish?

MAN. Jane, I—

JANE. You, too. Line up.

(MAN goes U.C. so it is DEXTER, PAUL, and MAN in a row.)

JANE. There. (*Moves back above desk.*) I am right. I knew I'd seen you before.

PAUL. Magazine cover? *Health and Fitness*? *Physiques*? One of them?

JANE. No. I've seen you in many a line-up.

MAN. A police line-up?

JANE. At the department. I've seen him lined up with aliens, dope dealers from Colombia, muggers—

MAN. Then he's the big guy you're after?

PAUL. No, not me.

JANE. Right, not you. If I've seen him in that many line-ups then he's a stand-in from the department.

MAN. He's another agent?

JANE. Where do you work, Paul?

PAUL. (*Drops his guise and goes above the sofa to Kitty.*) Not in the Pentagon. I'm with—well, I can't say.

KITTY. We're partners but if I did see him on the road for real, I would have picked him up. (*Her arm through his.*) He's so cute.

PAUL. Boy, this is a relief. I couldn't do that fitness bit much longer. My knees ache, my back hurts, and I'm dying for a cigarette.

MAN. So all of you are government employees? You all wear white hats?

(THEY all nod agreement and DEXTER moves above sofa.)

JANE. (*Crosses C.*) Not all. There is a black hat here.

DEXTER. Who?

JANE. We are all sent here because there is a big payoff due tonight but we don't know for what.

PAUL. Dope. Smuggling? Who knows?

JANE. The mastermind rented this place knowing it would be out of the way and uncrowded.

KITTY. Yeah, like the Pentagon at Happy Hour.

JANE. He had come here as a guest and left the plates.

DEXTER. Plates?

VERLA. But all the china is K-Mart.

JANE. The messenger to collect the money and hand over the plates was shot and—

WILMA. Then he never got here?

JANE. Before he died he said, "a bagful of money buys a handful of money."

PAUL. Anyone here do crosswords?

JANE. (*Crosses to shelves.*) It didn't make sense till I saw the titles of the movies here on tape.

SYLVIA. What, *Pennies From Heaven*?

PAUL. *How To Steal a Million*?

JANE. This one. (*Pulls out a movie.*) *A Fistful of Dollars.*

DEXTER. That old Clint Eastwood one?

KITTY. The Italian Western?

JANE. That's the clue and look what's inside instead of the tape. (*Goes C. and tips out the two plates.*) Plates. Printing plates.

DEXTER. (*Goes to her.*) For printing money, counterfeit money?

JANE. But Kitty gave away the real clue.

KITTY. I did?

JANE. It's a foreign movie so these are for a foreign country to pick up. Counterfeiting is getting too hot over here right now so these are up for sale. Didn't we all get the same interoffice memo? We know these are going out of the country.

SYLVIA. (*Rises and goes U.C.*) So someone here is ready to pay off a bundle for those?

WILMA. (*Rises.*) One of us?

JANE. But we're all good guys, aren't we?

KITTY. Are we?

JANE. Jack, get the suitcase from the closet. (*HE doesn't move.*) Jack!

KITTY. That's you.

MAN. Yes. I keep forgetting. (*Gets suitcase from closet.*)

JANE. He really doesn't know who he is?

SYLVIA. It's not an act?

JANE. It's classic functional amnesia. Here are the plates. (*Puts them on the desk.*) Jack, open the suitcase.

MAN. You're sure?

JANE. Yes. (*HE opens it on the sofa.*) And that's the money. Thousands of dollars! Nondeclarable income! Our government doesn't own it! No one does! It's up for grabs! Go on and take it!

(*THEY all rush for the money except VERLA who rises and picks up the plates.*)

MAN. (*Goes to Jane.*) What are you doing? Where's your trap?

JANE. It's just been sprung. (*Loudly to others.*) Hold it right there!

(*THEY all stop and turn to her.*)

JANE. There's your answer.

MAN. Where?

JANE. (*Points at Verla.*) Right there! All of you went for the money but she went for the plates.

VERLA. They're more valuable.

JANE. Only the person who brought the suitcase of money knows it is counterfeit.

SYLVIA. This is counterfeit? Damn! (*Drops her pack of money.*)

JANE. (*To Verla.*) So I knew one of you had made the money and kept the real payoff for yourself.

KITTY. It's true. There is no honor among thieves.

JANE. And there is dirty pool among crooks.

VERLA. (*As JANE crosses up behind her.*) You're wrong. I'm with you. I was sent here to help find the mastermind not double-cross him. What do you think I am?

JANE. (*From behind her in quick loud voice, SHE speaks German.*) Bist du politzei? (Means, "Are you a cop?")

VERLA. (*Snaps up straight and speaks back rapidly.*) Nein. Ich bin oberst—(*Means, "No I am a Chief—"*)

JANE. There!

VERLA. Verdammmte! (*Means "Damn!"*)

(*The following five lines of dialogue are spoken simultaneously.*)

KITTY. It's you!

SYLVIA. Damn foreigners!

WILMA. I didn't believe that sheriff bit.

DEXTER. It would be a woman after all.

PAUL. You're very good.

MAN. Jane, you did it. First the money and then speaking with forked tongue. Great!

JANE. (*To Verla as SHE goes left of desk.*) Now you tell us who is selling the plates or we'll turn you over to your boss at home and let him know you were double-crossing him.

DEXTER. And your life won't be worth a plugged pfennig ...

SYLVIA. Or drachma.

WILMA. Or ruble or whatever.

JANE. Or you can stay here in our witness protection program.

VERLA. I can't speak. This place is bugged, isn't it?

SYLVIA. Dexter and I thought it was and that's why we put on this married act all evening.

VERLA. (*Goes above desk.*) I won't say the name aloud but I'll write it down.

MAN. It's not me, is it?

VERLA. No, you're just a red herring. You car had a flat. I stopped to help and mugged you. Just a side-line of mine.

MAN. Then who am I?

VERLA. How the hell do I know? (*Takes wallet from her jacket or apron.*) Here's your wallet.

JANE. (*As SHE goes to Man.*) Write the name Verla.

VERLA. I'm writing. (*SHE does so at desk.*)

MAN. (*Opens wallet.*) I'm too nervous to do this.

JANE. (*Takes wallet.*) I'll do it.

SYLVIA. He's not Roger Lenox, of course.

WILMA. Or Leonard Mulwray.

KITTY. Or Willis Buttram.

DEXTER. Or Verla's Milton Roderman.

MAN. Then who am I?

JANE. (*Hands him his driver's license.*) Here's your driver's license. Your name is—

MAN. (*Looks.*) Jack Lister!

KITTY. (*To Jane.*) You were right. How did you know?

JANE. You were sent here by the department. You're one of us.

MAN. I am?

JANE. We drove up together. When we had the flat I went for help and that's when Verla found you.

MAN. I'm a good guy. Get me a white hat.

JANE. Now to find out the name of the mastermind. Verla—

MAN. I'd feel better if someone held a gun on her.

JANE. Who has a gun?

(ALL shake their heads.)

JANE. One of you must.

MAN. Why haven't you escaped?

VERLA. Where to? You'll give me a new identity and, who knows, maybe I'll be a legit sheriff somewhere else.

MAN. *(Looking in wallet.)* Look at this.

JANE. What?

MAN. Your picture, Jane. Your photograph is in my wallet and in a bathing suit. Twice, no, three times.

JANE. And why not? We are what is known as an item.

KITTY. It's a Harlequin Romance.

MAN. You and I—wait a minute. *(Looks at photo again.)* This is in front of the Lincoln Memorial and we were having lunch and you made tuna fish sandwiches and chocolate cup

cakes and I hate chocolate and—it's coming back,
my life is returning!

DEXTER. (*Moves in.*) Enough of the romance.
Who is the mastermind?

SYLVIA. What did Verla write?

VERLA. (*Hands over the paper.*) Here. And
he's big. Very big.

PAUL. (*Crosses in to Kitty.*) Is he in our own
government?

(*THEY all crowd around Jane and Man.*)

JANE. (*Holds the note.*) No! It can't be!

(*The following five lines of dialogue are spoken
simultaneously.*)

KITTY. Who is it?
SYLVIA. Let me see.
PAUL. Come on, Jane.
DEXTER. We have a right to see it.
MAN. He must be big!

JANE. Here.

(*THEY all look in unison.
The following dialogue is spoken
simultaneously.*)

MAN. I remember him. I remember everything now.

KITTY. Geez, I used to date him.

SYLVIA. I had lunch with him at the Shoreham last week.

DEXTER. And I beat him at squash. I should have known.

VERLA. I knew you'd be surprised.

WILMA. Wait till the President hears of this.

JANE. It will make *60 Minutes*.

(THEY continue as:)

CURTAIN

PROPERTY PLOT

ACT I

Preset: phone, answering machine, pad and
pencils, small phone book on desk
Doormat with key under it outside front door
Set of book covers glued together, medical
directory, video tapes on shelves

Down Right:
Flashlight (SYLVIA.
Flashlight (DEXTER)
Purse and topcoat (SYLVIA)
Pile of different colored towels and washcloths
(VERLA)
Geranium and pot (MAN)
Sheets and pillowcases (VERLA)
Small suitcase (SYLVIA)
Small suitcase (DEXTER)
Small listening device (SYLVIA)
Backpack (PAUL)
Suitcase and purse (KITTY)
Suitcase and purse (WILMA)

Off Up Right:
Light bulb (VERLA)
Wallet with money (DEXTER)
Small suitcase filled with wrapped money
(JANE)

Off Up Left: (kitchen):
25 watt light bulb (VERLA)

Off Up Left (Bathroom):
Damp cloth (MAN)

Small hand mirror (MAN)

ACT II, Scene 1:
Off Down Right:
Bag of Trail Mix (PAUL)

Off Up Right:
25 watt bulb (KITTY)
Lipstick (KITTY)

Scene 2:
Off Up Left:
Wallet with photos, license, etc. (VERLA)

On Shelves:
Video box with two printer's plates inside

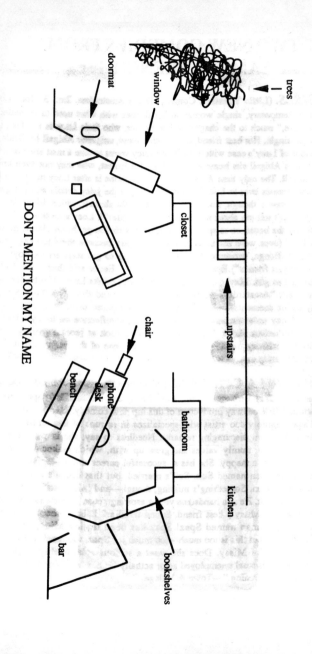

DON'T MENTION MY NAME

trees

window

doormat

closet

upstairs

chair

phone
desk
bench

bathroom

kitchen

bar

bookshelves

***FAST* (**

Lewis is
"healthy
easy—anc
deeply en
him up, w
she exists
date, whe
with envy
nuts ("If y
take the b
will marry
takes up
Sidney ("
doesn't *w*
can't hav
"Brilliantl
laughs . .
confusion
chaos]. Pa
Amsterdar

ADVIC

Carter Be
in the deli
Missy, an
videos, ad
from the
courant, b
life with
Missy fro
is, until sh
also the b
best frien
unmarried
possibly,
bourgeois
funny ...